FACT OR FICTION: RESEARCHING THE CAUSES OF

THE AMERICAN CIVIL WAR

TAYLER COLE

PowerKiDS press™

NEW YORK

Published in 2019 by The Rosen Publishing Group, Inc.
29 East 21st Street, New York, NY 10010

Editor: Therese Shea
Book Design: Rachel Rising

Photo Credits: Cover, p. 5 Stock Montage/Archive Photos/Getty Images; Cover, pp. 1, 3, 4, 5, 6, 8, 9, 10, 11, 12, 13, 14, 15, 16, 18, 20, 22, 23, 24, 26, 28, 29, 30, 31, 32 Lyubov_Nazarova/Shutterstock.com; pp. 4, 8, 10, 14, 22, 26, 28, (insert) kontur-vid/Shutterstock.com; p. 6 Historical/ Corbis Historical/Getty Images; p. 7 f11photo/Shutterstock.com; p. 9 Everett Historical/Shutterstock.com; p. 11 Rainer Lesniewski/Shutterstock.com; pp. 12,17, 19, 21, 25 (background) Reinhold Leitner/Shutterstock.com;p. 12 https://commons.wikimedia.org/wiki/File:1837_Liberator_Cornhill_Boston. png; p. 12 https://commons.wikimedia.org/wiki/File:1831_Liberator.jpg; p. 13 https://commons.wikimedia.org/wiki/ File:Robert_Edward_Lee.jpg; pp. 15, 17 (documents), 21, 25, 27 Courtesy of the Library of Congress; p. 19 https:// commons.wikimedia.org/wiki/File:The_seceding_South_Carolina_delegation_(Boston_Public_Library).jpg; p. 20 https://commons.wikimedia.org/wiki/File:Confederate_%27Stars_and_Bars%27_Flag,_captured_at_Columbia,_ South_Carolina_-_Wisconsin_Veterans_Museum_-_DSC02996.JPG; p. 23 https://commons.wikimedia.org/wiki/ File:Abraham_Lincoln_O-55,_1861-crop.jpg; p. 29 Jose Gil/Shutterstock.com.

Cataloging-in-Publication Data

Names: Cole, Tayler.
Title: Fact or fiction? researching the causes of the American Civil War / Tayler Cole.
Description: New York : PowerKids Press, 2019. | Series: Project learning through American history | Includes glossary and index.
Identifiers: LCCN ISBN 9781538330609 (pbk.) | ISBN 9781538330593 (library bound) | ISBN 9781538330616 (6 pack)
Subjects: LCSH: United States--History--Civil War, 1861-1865--Causes--Juvenile literature.
Classification: LCC E459.C65 2019 | DDC 973.7'11--dc23

Manufactured in the United States of America

CPSIA Compliance Information: Batch #CS18PKFor further information contact Rosen Publishing, New York, New York at 1-800-237-9932.

CONTENTS

QUESTIONING THE CAUSES

The American Civil War was fought from 1861 to 1865 between the United States and the 11 Southern states that left the Union to form the Confederate States of America. It remains the deadliest war in terms of American deaths.

Although the conflict was more than 150 years ago, Americans still debate, or argue, about its causes. Did Northern soldiers give their lives because they were morally against slavery? Did Southern states secede, or leave the Union, over states' rights? While the Civil War was officially fought between the Union and the Confederacy, there were

Firsthand Accounts

Primary sources are writings, art, photographs, records, and objects that were created by people who lived during the time you're studying. They're a great place to start when you're researching an event. Researching isn't just studying what other people think. It means examining facts and making your own conclusions. Secondary sources are sources created after the time you're studying. If you want to separate fiction from facts, would it be better to use primary sources or secondary sources?

By using primary sources, you can learn to separate facts from fiction passed down about the Civil War and other major historical events. This book will show you how to do this.

multiple viewpoints on both sides of the war. As you read, think about each side's experiences before and after the war and how these perspectives, or viewpoints, might have shaped how the history was recorded.

NORTHERN AND SOUTHERN DIFFERENCES

The North and South were very different places to live before the Civil War. In the South, most people made their money through farming. The warm climate allowed for a long growing season. Some Southerners owned large farms called plantations and became rich through **cash crops** such as tobacco and cotton. Most plantation owners owned many slaves and relied on their labor to make large profits. Plantation owners began looking west for more land to increase their profits.

Slaves often lived in poor housing. Contrast the plantation house you see here with the living quarters of these slaves in Georgia, shown on page 6.

The Northern states increasingly relied on trading and manufacturing for their economy. Large factories made products such as paper and cloth quickly and cheaply. Many **immigrants** worked in these factories for low wages. Slavery gradually decreased in the North, and many freed slaves lived and worked there.

FACT OR FICTION? ALL SOUTHERNERS OWNED SLAVES

White Southerners are often grouped together. Did they all own slaves? This is definitely fiction. In 1860, the United States took a **census**. The historical record produced tells us less than 50 percent of white Southerners owned slaves. In some states, it was less than 25 percent. And even fewer could afford to own multiple slaves.

The Pastor's Opinion

Many Southern church officials preached their approval of slavery. They used stories in the Bible to back up their opinions. Pastor Samuel Dunwody of South Carolina said, "God has authorized the practice of slavery. . . . Therefore, slavery is not a moral evil." Think about Pastor Dunwody's audience. How do you think his position as a pastor would have affected people's opinions of slavery?

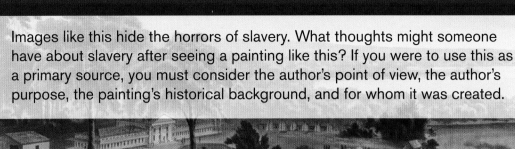

Images like this hide the horrors of slavery. What thoughts might someone have about slavery after seeing a painting like this? If you were to use this as a primary source, you must consider the author's point of view, the author's purpose, the painting's historical background, and for whom it was created.

The South had a firm set of social classes. Poor Southerners felt more comfortable about their low social standing because they knew they weren't the bottom group. They also held on to the belief that, if they worked hard enough, they could become rich and own slaves, too. When they defended the practice of slavery, they were defending the better life they hoped to have someday.

9

FACT OR FICTION? TARIFFS CAUSED SECESSION

Some people believe high **tariffs** hurt the Southern economy and were the reason the states seceded. Historical **documents** show there was a new tariff act put in place in 1857, thanks largely to Southern congressmen. This act lowered rates and helped the economy rather than hurt it. Another tariff act, raising rates, was passed in 1861, but the Southern states left before they could attempt to block its passage. So, why *did* the states leave the Union if not because of tariffs?

Mississippi Explains

*Mississippi's 1861 declaration about its secession states: "Our position is thoroughly identified with the **institution** of slavery—the greatest material interest of the world. Its labor supplies the product which constitutes by far the largest and most important portions of **commerce** of the earth." Why did state leaders view slavery as so important? What do you think Mississippians feared might happen if slavery were abolished?*

Southerners' wealth was tied closely to the institution of slavery, while the North was developing an industrial economy. The map below shows how divided the country was during the American Civil War.

UNION STATES WITHOUT SLAVERY   CONFEDERATE STATES

UNION STATES WITH SLAVERY   TERRITORIES

As some states seceded, their leaders wrote documents explaining their exit. They gave different reasons, but none mentioned unfair tariffs. Instead, they stated that slavery was necessary to their economy and the structure of their society. They feared the Union would abolish, or get rid of, slavery and destroy the Southern way of life.

FACT OR FICTION? SLAVERY WAS A MORAL ISSUE

It's true many **abolitionists** felt strongly about the moral evils of slavery. William Lloyd Garrison was the publisher of the *Liberator*, an antislavery newspaper. He thought if people could be persuaded of the immorality of slavery, they would turn against it. In an 1854 speech, he said, "When I say that freedom is of God and slavery is of the devil, I mean just what I say."

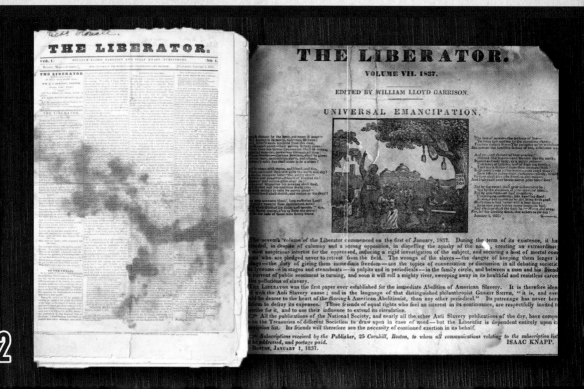

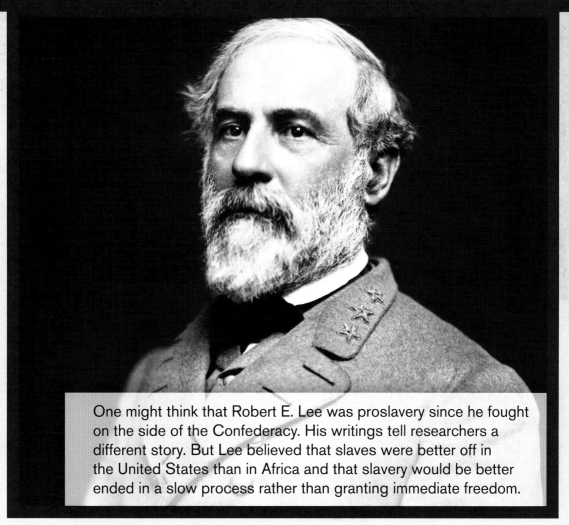

One might think that Robert E. Lee was proslavery since he fought on the side of the Confederacy. His writings tell researchers a different story. But Lee believed that slaves were better off in the United States than in Africa and that slavery would be better ended in a slow process rather than granting immediate freedom.

But it's not true that all Northerners agreed with him. And it's also fiction that all Southerners thought slavery was good. In fact, future Confederate general Robert E. Lee wrote in a letter in 1856: "There are few, I believe, in this enlightened age, who will not acknowledge that slavery as an institution is a moral and political evil."

CONGRESSIONAL COMPROMISES

In the mid-1800s, American leaders worried about a power struggle in Congress. Leaders in the states in which slavery was allowed feared that if they became outnumbered in Congress, they would lose the power to protect their interests. As states were added to the Union, this seemed possible. In 1820, Congress passed the Missouri **Compromise** to keep a balance of power between Northern and Southern congressmen. Maine was added as a free state, and Missouri was added as a slave state. Slavery was banned from future territories or states north of Missouri's southern border.

Calhoun Criticizes Compromise

The Missouri Compromise was just the first compromise on the road to the Civil War. It kept the peace for a time, but John C. Calhoun, a Southern lawmaker, wrote in a letter: "The discussion on the Missouri question has undoubtedly contributed to weaken in some degree the attachment of our southern and western people to the Union." Why might debating the compromises have weakened the Union rather than strengthening it?

The Fugitive Slave Act of 1850 was part of the Compromise of 1850. It forced Northerners to aid in the return of escaped slaves to the South. This illustration was created in response to this measure. How do you think the artist viewed the act?

In 1849, California requested to enter the Union as a free state. Congress created the Compromise of 1850 to address this addition to the Union. California was added as a free state, but the North had to make new compromises.

FACT OR FICTION? SECESSION WAS OVER STATES' RIGHTS

The term "federalism" refers to the sharing of power between the federal and state governments. This is how the U.S. government works. The Constitution, the highest law in the land, gives certain powers to the president, Congress, and the Supreme Court. It allows the states other powers. This system was put in place so the states could have a say in how they were governed but work together through the federal government to handle certain issues. It was important to the states to have power, since they held little as colonies under England.

In truth, the South had much power in the federal government in the years leading up to the war. Leaders saw no need to call for their states' rights until the mid-1800s.

In 1850, states that would later become the Confederacy met in Nashville, Tennessee. Among their resolutions was that they had a right to secede if non-slaveholding states disregarded the Constitution and its provisions regarding slavery.

Did Southern states leave the Union because their rights were being denied? In the years before the Civil War, South Carolina's leaders were angry that Northern states ignored federal law by not returning fugitive slaves to their owners. They also were upset that New York forbade visiting Southerners from bringing their slaves to the state.

South Carolina addressed these issues in its declaration of secession, stating: "But an increasing hostility on the part of the non-slaveholding States to the institution of slavery, has led to a disregard of their obligations [duties]. . . . In many of these States the fugitive is discharged from service or labor claimed. . . . In the State of New York even the right of transit [travel] for a slave has been denied by her tribunals [courts]."

The rights of the Northern states to stand against slavery weren't important to South Carolina. Instead, South Carolina disapproved of these states refusing to "fulfill their constitutional obligations."

HARPER'S WEEKLY.

A JOURNAL OF CIVILIZATION

Vol. IV.—No. 208.]   NEW YORK, SATURDAY, DECEMBER 22, 1860.   [PRICE FIVE CENTS.

Entered according to Act of Congress, in the Year 1860, by Harper & Brothers, in the Clerk's Office of the District Court for the Southern District of New York.

KEITT.   CHESNUT.   M'QUEEN.   HAMMOND.   BONHAM.
BOYCE.   ASHMORE.   MILES.

THE SECEDING SOUTH CAROLINA DELEGATION.—[PHOTOGRAPHED BY BRADY.]

Many claim that the Southern states left the Union because they feared the federal government would abolish slavery across the nation. They maintain the states only wanted the slavery issue to remain the choice of each state. However, the Confederate States of America, the nation comprised of the seceded states, denied its states the right to choose whether to allow slavery. In its Constitution of the Confederate States, adopted March 11, 1861, it stated: "In all such territory the institution of negro slavery, as it now exists in the Confederate States, shall be recognized and protected by Congress."

Confederate "Stars and Bars" flag

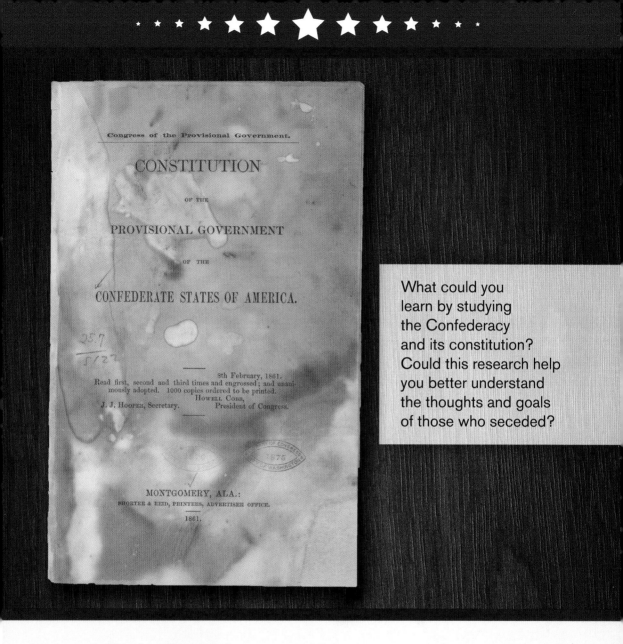

Congress of the Provisional Government.

CONSTITUTION

OF THE

PROVISIONAL GOVERNMENT

OF THE

CONFEDERATE STATES OF AMERICA.

8th February, 1861.
Read first, second and third times and engrossed; and unanimously adopted. 1000 copies ordered to be printed.
HOWELL COBB,
J. J. HOOPER, Secretary.   President of Congress.

MONTGOMERY, ALA.:
SHORTER & REID, PRINTERS, ADVERTISER OFFICE.

1861.

What could you learn by studying the Confederacy and its constitution? Could this research help you better understand the thoughts and goals of those who seceded?

To the Confederacy, the idea of states' rights didn't extend to slavery because the institution was so rooted in the Southern way of life. Instead, slavery was cemented in the Confederacy through its constitution.

FACT OR FICTION? LINCOLN WANTED TO ABOLISH SLAVERY

After Abraham Lincoln's election in 1860, many Southerners were afraid he would abolish slavery. Lincoln hadn't publicly stated that he would or wouldn't. He was clear about some issues, though. He wrote in a letter in 1861: "I am for no compromise which assists or permits the extension of the institution [of slavery] on soil owned by the nation." However, while he stated he believed slavery

Fear for the Future

Alexander Stephens told Georgians they had nothing to fear from Lincoln: "He can do nothing unless he is backed by power in Congress. The House of Representatives is largely in the majority against him. In the Senate he will also be powerless." The U.S. federal government consists of the president, Congress, and the Supreme Court. A system of checks and balances prevents one branch from obtaining too much power. Why wouldn't this knowledge have calmed the South's fears about Lincoln?

Lincoln was clear in a letter that his goal was to keep the nation united: "My opinion is that no state can, in any way lawfully, get out of the Union, without the consent of the others; and that it is the duty of the President, and other government functionaries, to run the machine as it is."

was wrong, he gave no indication that he would work to remove it from the South.

Lincoln wrote Alexander Stephens, a friend and Georgia representative, "Do the people in the South really entertain fears that a Republican administration would, directly or indirectly, interfere with their slaves? If they do, I wish to assure you . . . there is no cause for such fears."

SOUTHERN SECESSION

On December 20, 1860, South Carolina seceded from the Union. Ten more states followed over the next few months. However, there was still no active threat to slavery. Before Lincoln's **inauguration**, a senator proposed an amendment to the Constitution that promised the federal government couldn't abolish slavery at any point. This amendment wasn't ratified, or approved, by enough states, however. That was in part because many Southern states had already seceded.

Only in April 1861, when the Confederacy seized a federal fort in South Carolina, did Lincoln send in federal forces. Even still, his goal was simply to keep the country together. He wrote to Horace Greeley of the *New-York Tribune* in 1862, "If I could save the Union without freeing any slave, I would do it; and if I could save it by freeing all the slaves, I would do it."

On April 12, 1861, Confederate forces opened fire on Fort Sumter. The next day, Major Robert Anderson surrendered the fort.

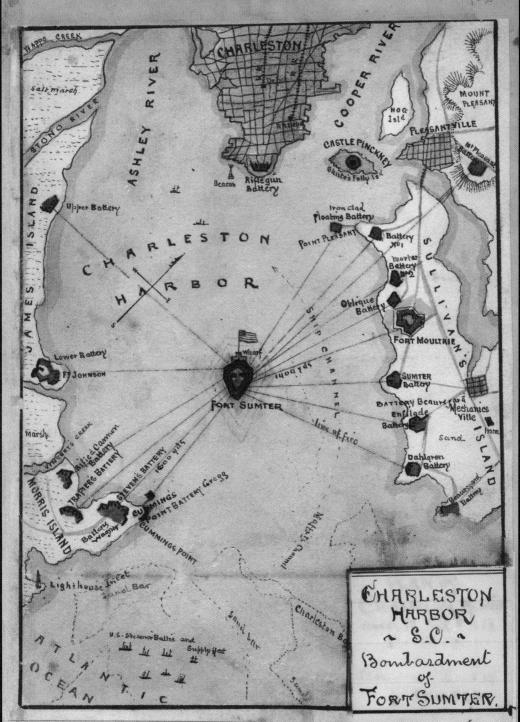

CHARLESTON

COOPER RIVER

ASHLEY RIVER

STONO RIVER

WAPPO CREEK

salt march

CHARLESTON HARBOR

JAMES ISLAND

Upper Battery

Beacon
Riflegun Battery

CASTLE PINCKNEY
Shute's Folly Is.

HOG Isld

MOUNT PLEASANT

PLEASANTVILLE

Mt Pleasant Battery

Iron clad Floating Battery

Point Pleasant

Battery No 1

Mortar Battery No 2

Oblique Battery

Fort Moultrie

SULLIVANS ISLAND

Lower Battery
Ft Johnson

Ship Channel 1400 feet

Sumter Battery

FORT SUMTER
Wharf

line of fire

Battery Beauregard
Enfilade Battery

Mechanics Ville

Marsh

Vinegar's creek

Battie a Cannon Battery
Trapiers Battery

Stevens Battery 1600 yds

Cummings
Point Battery Gregg

Battery Wagner

CUMMINGS POINT

MORRIS ISLAND

sand
from

Dahlgren Battery

Beauregard Battery

Lighthouse Inlet
Sand Bar

Sand Bar

North Channel

Swash Channel

Charleston Bar

Sand

U.S. Steamer Baltic and Supply fleet

ATLANTIC OCEAN

CHARLESTON
HARBOR
~ S.C. ~
Bombardment
of
FORT SUMTER.

HISTORICAL BIAS

History is created by **analyzing** records of the past such as written documents, objects, and spoken accounts. This can lead to disagreements, because each historian may understand these sources in a different way. Documents and other sources can also be **biased** in themselves. In addition, the victors of war and those in power tend to be the writers of history. All this means that history isn't always about facts.

Apply this knowledge to the Civil War. Who was the winner, and how would they want history to regard them? Did the losers of the Civil War have any influence on the historical accounts? Could more recent events change or reshape the way Civil War history is viewed?

Head to the Library

The Library of Congress is the largest library in the world. It's run by the federal government. The library gathers and organizes primary and secondary sources from all over the world. You can visit www.loc.gov to learn more. States and colleges also collect sources and share them with the public. Why would these places be trustworthy sources for your research? Could these collections of information be biased?

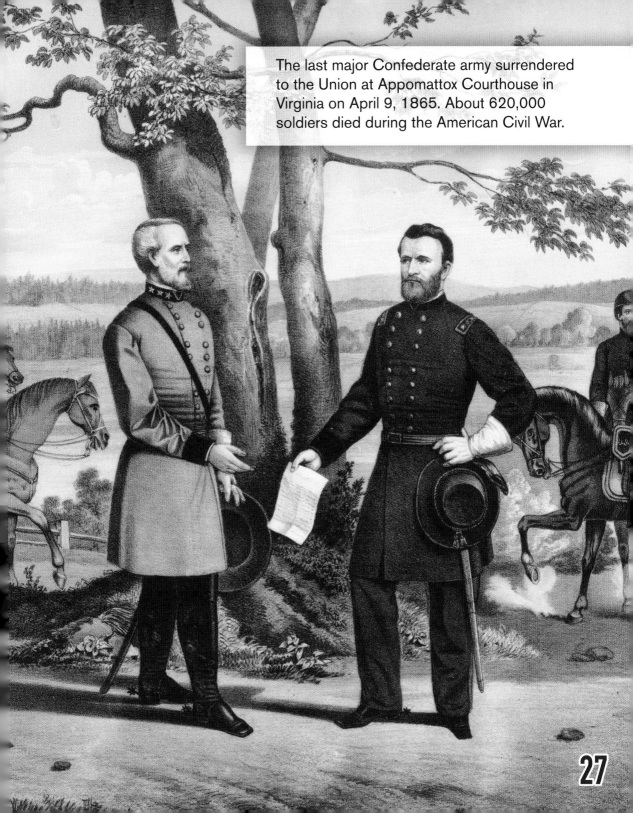

The last major Confederate army surrendered to the Union at Appomattox Courthouse in Virginia on April 9, 1865. About 620,000 soldiers died during the American Civil War.

DIFFERENT VIEWPOINTS

In 2010, a group held a ball in Charleston, South Carolina, to celebrate the 150th anniversary of the state's secession. About 300 people joined the party. Many were the descendants of Confederate soldiers, and most agreed that secession had nothing to do with slavery.

"For us the secession is not about a racial issue," said Michael Givens, a member of the group Sons of Confederate Veterans. "We are not celebrating slavery, we are celebrating the courage . . . of the people who were prepared to go out and defend their homes."

What If?

"What would happen if Japanese Americans decided to have a ball to celebrate Pearl Harbor?" asked Reverend Nelson Rivers, one of the South Carolina ball's protestors. In 1941, Japan bombed Pearl Harbor in Hawaii, leading to the United States' entry into World War II. What do you think Rivers meant by his comment? Would a Japanese American celebration be similar to or different than the South Carolina ball?

How do you think people's **heritage** affects their views of the Civil War and life in the South in the mid-1800s?

Outside the event, about 150 people protested the ball. Some of these people were descended from slaves. Why do you think these protestors were upset by the celebration?

REMEMBERING THE CIVIL WAR

History can be rewritten over time. Sometimes new information is found or historians write about events from a new perspective. Newly discovered facts and multiple viewpoints are a good thing, but they can change the way history is viewed.

People often create monuments in the years after a war to pay respect to those who fought. More than 700 Confederate monuments were constructed after the American Civil War. Most weren't raised until years, sometimes many years, later. In modern times, the monuments may anger people who believe they're glorifying slavery and people who supported it. These people want the monuments removed. Others disagree. Research one of these **controversial** monuments. Find out when, why, and by whom it was erected, if possible. Use the facts you find to decide which side you agree with.

GLOSSARY

abolitionist: A person who wants to stop slavery.

analyze: To study something closely and carefully.

biased: To have a prejudice, or generally unfair feeling, in favor of something or against something.

cash crop: A crop produced for its commercial value.

census: The official process of counting the number of people in a country, city, or town and collecting information about them.

commerce: The large-scale buying and selling of goods and services.

compromise: An agreement in which each person or group gives up something in order to end a dispute.

controversial: Likely to give rise to disagreement.

document: A formal piece of writing.

heritage: The traditions and beliefs that are part of the history of a group or nation.

immigrant: A person who comes to a country to live there.

inauguration: The act of introducing a newly elected official into a job or position with a formal ceremony.

institution: A custom, practice, or law that is accepted and used by many people.

tariff: A tax on goods coming into or leaving a country.

INDEX

WEBSITES

Due to the changing nature of Internet links, PowerKids Press has developed an online list of websites related to the subject of this book. This site is updated regularly. Please use this link to access the list: www.powerkidslinks.com/pltam/fact